This Bunny Book!
belongs
to
yeha Park

bunnies at play

bunnies at play

Sophie Bevan

photography by Dan Duchars

RYLAND
PETERS
& SMALL
LONDON NEW YORK

Designer *Sarah Walden*

Editor *Sharon Ashman*

Location and Picture Researcher *Emily Westlake*

Production *Patricia Harrington*

Art Director *Gabriella Le Grazie*

Publishing Director *Alison Starling*

First published in Great Britain in 2004
by Ryland Peters & Small
Kirkman House
12–14 Whitfield Street
London W1T 2RP
www.rylandpeters.com

10 9 8 7 6 5 4 3 2 1

Text, design and photographs
© Ryland Peters & Small 2004

ISBN 1 84172 615 X

A CIP record for this book is available from the
British Library.

Printed in China

contents

irresistible rabbits

charmed

With his floppity ears, cotton-ball tail and twitching whiskers, it's impossible to see the rabbit as anything but cute. Yet the bunny is an important symbol of luck, fertility and wicked cunning. This fluffy little ball of fur demands our respect.

Who could be immune to the charms of the rabbit? His true purpose in life is surely to be worshipped. The rabbit was first domesticated by medieval monks in France, initially to be used for food and fur. However, by the fourteenth century, the cuddly ones had won over the religious institutions, where monks and nuns kept them in hutches, or even in their own chambers. In 1387, the English clerical reformer William of Wykeham had had enough of this idolatry, and lamented that nuns paid more heed to their rabbits than to the church!

'The reason we have two ears and
only one mouth is that we may hear
more and speak less.'

Zeno (335–264 BC)

'Their morals are of the loosest description.'

John Everett Millais (1829–96) on rabbits

In Britain there seems to have been some confusion as to whether rabbits brought good or bad luck. Certainly, saying 'white rabbit' three times at the beginning of the month could herald the arrival of gifts within the next four weeks. Yet in many parts of England, a man meeting a rabbit on his way to work would turn straight round and go back to bed! In other parts, it was lucky to meet a rabbit, but unlucky if it crossed your path. And a fisherman couldn't set sail if a rabbit had been caught in his nets on the dock overnight.

worship me

In ancient China, the rabbit was a mystical figure linked with the Moon. In one story, Buddha asked the rabbit for food. Having nothing to offer, the bunny leapt into the fire and cooked himself for the hungry traveller. As a reward, Buddha exalted the rabbit to the lofty position of the Moon, where he can still be seen if you look carefully into the night sky.

'Princes have big ears which hear far and near.'

Elizabeth I

(1533–1603)

the trickster

prince of mischief

As we have seen, the rabbit has long been worshipped, yet rabbit-spirits were not always benevolent givers of life. Rather, the rabbit is a cunning little trickster-spirit. It would seem he constantly has a new scam up his sleeve, so it's not hard to see why he's associated with the magician's hat!

'Wish for rabbits, or white mice or chocolate.'

Edith Nesbit, *Five Children and It*, 1902

The Anglo-Saxon goddess, Eastre, was believed to have transformed a bird into a rabbit that laid colourful eggs each Spring – an image clearly recognizable in the Easter bunny. But don't be fooled by those floppy ears and the basket of eggs – the rabbit is invariably looking after number one! From the Zambian hare Kalulu to Brer Rabbit and the all-American Bugs Bunny, rabbits have long been up to no good, outwitting lions, foxes, and – of course – Elmer Fudd.

'"Bother errands," said he, banging the door angrily behind him, and paying little heed to Mother Bunny as she cried to him to be good and return safely home.'

Harry Rountree, *The Story of Wicked Tim*, 1917

African folklore is littered with tales of the rabbit getting others into trouble – often for his own benefit. For example, there are tales of how he lost humankind their chance of immortality; of how he tricked the hippo and the elephant into a tug-of-war in order to impress a potential bride; and of how he cheated the lion out of his supper.

'"Didn't the fox never catch the rabbit,
Uncle Remus?" asked the little boy.'

Joel Chandler Harris, *Remus Tales*, 1881

gardener's foe

in the potting shed

A potent symbol of fertility from ancient Egypt to modern America, it seems unfair that the rabbit should be so despised by gardeners and farmers. Yet, whether it's the Romans or Elmer Fudd, it seems someone always has a bad word to say about the 'wotten wabbit'.

hungry bunny

Landowners weren't always so anti-rabbit. When bunnies first left their home on the Iberian peninsula, people fell over themselves to ensure the floppy-eared ones were well fed and cared for. The Romans built them vast landscaped areas called *leporaria*. In Britain complex warrens were built, complete with banks of sandy soil to provide the rabbits with well-drained burrows, and a healthy supply of dandelions, groundsel and parsley was kept on hand.

the food from your plate

The fresh green shoots on young trees, the first sign of tulips in Spring, and those beans you were looking forward to with your supper – rabbits have a habit of getting there first, leaving just their neat little teeth marks, like a good pair of pruning shears. If they put the same effort into trimming the lawn, they may

be more welcome in the garden. But the sight of two long ears poking out of the shrubbery, or of a white cotton tail disappearing into the hedge serves to remind you that the garden isn't solely for your enjoyment!

'The whole country is a mere rabbit warren.'

The fifth Earl of Albemarle (1794–1851)

Over 800 islands around the world have been invaded by rabbits, from burrowing bunnies threatening to topple the lighthouse on Washington's San Juan Island, to the Balearics, where natives were almost driven off their islands by the new colonizers! In eighteenth-century England, rabbits upset the navy by nibbling all the fresh shoots of young oak trees, leaving them short of wood for shipbuilding.

When it comes to vegetable thieves, everyone's favourites are those mischievous cousins Peter Rabbit and Benjamin Bunny in the tales of Beatrix Potter. They were forever outsmarting Mr McGregor to savour the delights of his garden or rescuing the Flopsy Bunnies from Mrs McGregor's kitchen. Benjamin H. Bouncer was the real-life rabbit on whom Benjamin Bunny was based. Beatrix Potter described her pet as a rascal, constantly getting into all kinds of mischief. However, it seems that 'Bounce' was more likely to be found feasting on hot buttered toast in the parlour and overturning teacups to the delight of young guests, than stealing carrots from the vegetable patch.

'Oh, John the rabbit, Yes, Ma'am
Got a mighty habit, Yes, Ma'am
Jumping in my garden, Yes Ma'am
Cutting down my cabbage, Yes Ma'am'

Traditional American folk song

rabbit rabbit

long-eared lover

Rabbits are the socialites of the four-legged world. They live in large groups and are never happier than when frolicking together. Of course, the rabbit's reputation as paramour is legendary – according to one estimate, a breeding pair could expand their population to 2,164,800 in just four years!

In the wild, rabbits live in groups of 70 or more in large warrens. However, attempts at living with other animals, be they dogs or cats, guinea pigs or hens, have met with mixed results. In coastal areas, wild rabbits often vie with birds for nests, and fierce puffins are known to evict bunnies from their sea-view burrows. The writer Oliver Goldsmith reported a rather different encounter between a rabbit and a bird, resulting in a feathery, furry offspring – half-rabbit, half-hen!

Despite his friendly nature, the rabbit – whether wild or tame – is unlikely to greet a new best friend with open arms. In fact, it is not unusual for fur to literally fly. Being a social animal, the rabbit is also a bit of a bureaucrat, and likes nothing better than establishing a pecking order. This usually involves some biting, bullying, head-butting, and eventually giving his new companion a thorough bath.

lap dog

Bunnies can be the most loving of pets and the most formidable of opponents. It would seem the rabbit has no concept of his diminutive size, and expects the whole animal kingdom to submit to his will. It's not unheard of for a dwarf breed to attack a large dog, or for a heavy lop-eared bunny to pin down a defenceless cat. However, once the family dog or cat knows his place, he makes a good friend and protector – as well as a useful hot-water bottle on a chilly afternoon.

'Animals are such agreeable
friends – they ask no questions;
they pass no criticisms.'

George Eliot (1819–80)

sweethearts

The history of the rabbit's relationship with humans is a chequered one, and who could blame the bunny if he were a little sceptical of our intentions? During the eighteenth and nineteenth centuries, it became very popular to keep rabbits in hutches. These tame bunnies came to be known as sweetheart rabbits – a sure sign of the degree of affection that was growing between owners and their new-found pets.

Now bunnies are among the most popular of pets, and have been moved out of their backyard hutches to take centre stage alongside Fido and Felix on the hearth rug. So, if you find the TV aerial has been chewed through, or the toilet paper used to redecorate

'Rabbits are most awfully tame sometimes.'
Edith Nesbit, *Story of the Amulet*, 1906

the bathroom, or your shoelaces have been carefully removed and hidden – you can be sure there is a bunny rabbit in the house!

'Happy enough to chat and play
With birds and rabbits and such as they.'

Charlotte Mew, *The Farmer's Bride*, 1916

The advent of the house-rabbit signals a new stage in the relationship between bunnies and humans. Surely it won't be long before no home is complete without a hoppity, floppity guardian of its own.

'He dropped his ears, set up his tail,
and left for San Francisco at a speed
which can only be described as a flash
and a vanish. Long after he was out of
sight we could hear him whiz.'

Mark Twain, on the jackass rabbit in
Roughing It, 1872

useful addresses

British Rabbit Council
Purefoy House
7 Kirkgate
Newark
Nottinghamshire
NG24 1AD
01636 676042
www.thebrc.org
The British Rabbit
Council promotes the
breeding and showing of
rabbits and helps pet
owners with the welfare
of their rabbits.

Fur & Feather magazine
Elder House
Chattisham
Ipswich
Suffolk IP8 3QE
01473 652789
www.furandfeather.co.uk
furandfeather@btinternet.
com
Magazine for small
livestock fans and
fanciers.

The House Rabbit Society
www.rabbit.org (USA)
An international non-
profit organization
which rescues rabbits
and educates the public
on rabbit care and
behaviour.

Rabbit Welfare
Association
PO Box 603
Horsham
West Sussex
RH13 5W
www.rabbitwelfare.co.uk
National Helpline:
01403 267658
A club for rabbit lovers in
the UK, promoting the
welfare of all pet rabbits.

acknowledgments

The publisher would like to thank all those who kindly
allowed us to photograph their rabbits:

Ann, Alan and Karen for all their help and advice

Terrie Lyons of Orchard Cottage
Bunnies & Rescue Centre

Everyone at *Fur & Feather* magazine

Thank you also to our models: Thomas,
Emily, Jamie, Josh and Kevin

Special thanks to:
Scallywags Petshop
& Grooming Parlour
816 Wickham Road
West Wickham
Kent CR0 8EB
020 8777 3440
*Dwarf Lops, French Lops,
and Mini Lops especially
bred for Scallywags*

Thanks to R. K. Alliston
for the kind loan of
gardening accessories:
R. K. Alliston
173 New Kings Road
London SW6 4SW
www.rkalliston.com
Mail order:
0845 130 5577